INDIAN
FOOD AND DRINK

V. P. (Hemant) Kanitkar

Wayland

FOOD AND DRINK

Chinese Food and Drink
French Food and Drink
Indian Food and Drink
Italian Food and Drink

First published in 1986 by
Wayland (Publishers) Ltd
61 Western Road, Hove,
East Sussex BN3 1JD, England

British Library Cataloguing in Publication Data
Kanitkar, V.P.
  Indian food and drink. — (Food and drink)
  1. Cookery, India   2. Beverages — India
  I. Title   II. Series
  641'.0954   TX724.5.I4

  ISBN 0-85078-897-8

Typeset by DP Press Ltd, Sevenoaks, Kent
Printed in Italy by G. Canale & C.S.p.A., Turin
Bound in Britain at The Bath Press, Avon

Cover   *A vegetable stall in Bombay's famous Crawford market.*

Picture Acknowledgements

The publishers would like to thank the following for their permission to reproduce copyright pictures: Anthony Blake 21, 24, 34; Cephas Picture Library 29; Bruce Coleman 38 (Charles Henneghien); Jimmy Holmes, Himalayan Images 4, 13, 26; Hutchison Library 12 (top), 16 (top), 35, 41, 42; VP (Hemant) Kanitkar 12 (bottom), 16 (bottom), 30 (top), 39 (top); Juliette Nicholson 15, 19, 20, 22, 28, 31, 32, 44; Christine Osborne *cover*, 8, 9, 23, 25, 27, 36, 40; Ann & Bury Peerless 7, 33, 37, Syndication International 43; TOPHAM 6, 13; Wayland Picture Library 7, 17 (Preben Kristensen). The maps on pages 5, 6 and 10 are by Malcolm S. Walker.

Contents

India and its people

India covers an area of 3,263,400 sq km (1,260,000 sq miles) and has a population of around 750 million. This vast land, which is as large as Western Europe, has many different climatic regions, with varied food and drink, styles of dress and languages. All the great religions are practised here, but over 80 per cent of the people follow the Hindu faith.

Hindi and English are the official languages of India, but in the states regional languages such as Punjabi, Gujarati, Bengali, Marathi or Tamil are also used. English, though widely used in the cities, is used by only about 4 per cent of the people. There are eighteen major languages in India and a large number of regional dialects.

The semi-circular range of high Himalaya mountains separates India from the rest of Asia, and its 4,800 km (3,000 mile) coastline is washed by the Arabian Sea, the

Small patches of fertile, snow-fed soil in the Himalayas near Ladakh.

Right *The Indian sub-continent covers an area as large as Western Europe.*

4

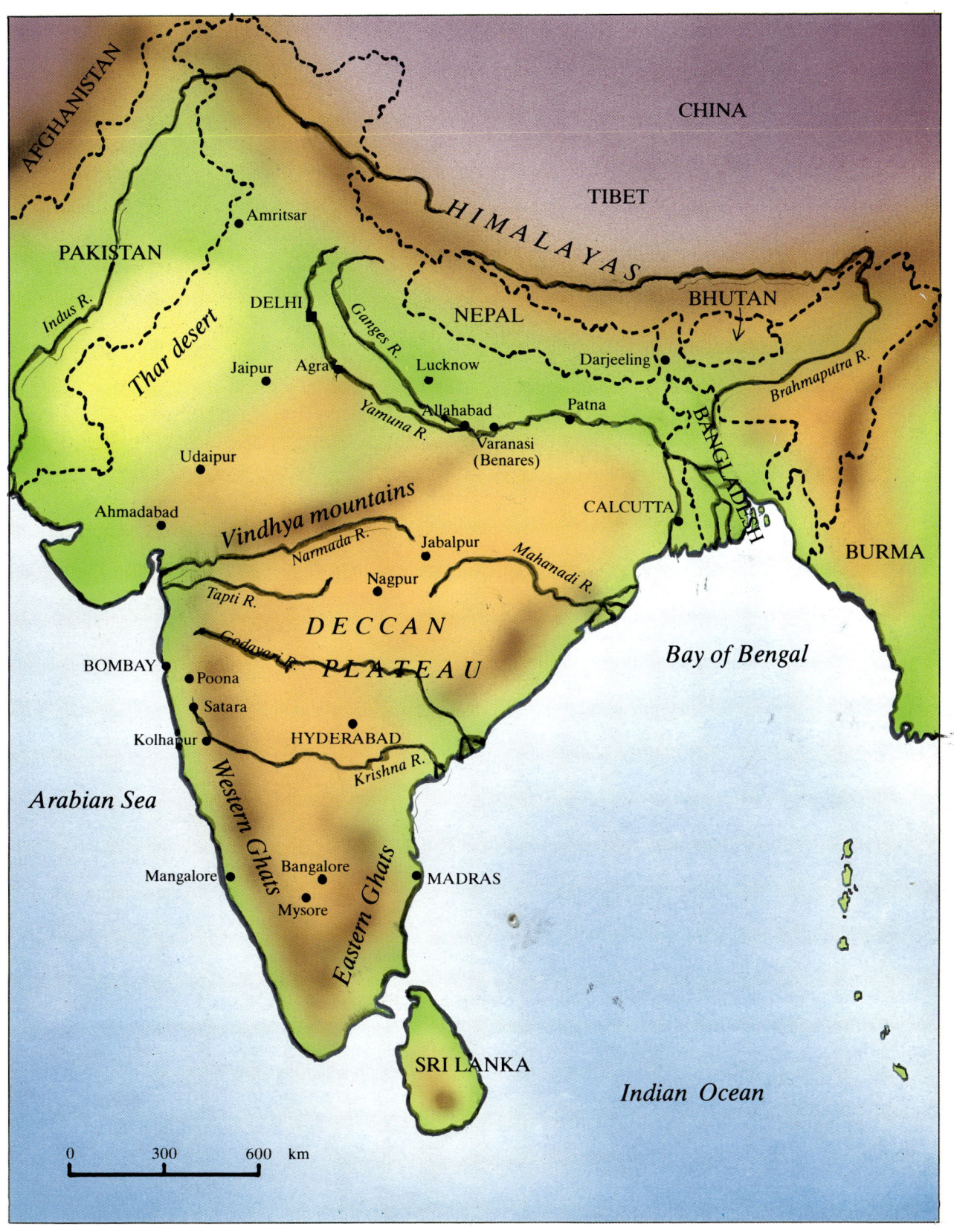

AFGHANISTAN

CHINA

TIBET

HIMALAYAS

PAKISTAN

• Amritsar

Indus R.

DELHI

NEPAL

BHUTAN

Ganges R.

Jaipur • • Agra

• Lucknow

Darjeeling •

Yamuna R.

Allahabad

Patna •

Brahmaputra R.

Thar desert

Udaipur •

Varanasi
(Benares)

BANGLADESH

Ahmadabad •

Vindhya mountains

CALCUTTA •

BURMA

Narmada R.

Jabalpur •

Mahanadi R.

Tapti R.

Nagpur •

DECCAN

Godavari R.

PLATEAU

Bay of Bengal

BOMBAY • • Poona
• Satara

Kolhapur • HYDERABAD •

Arabian Sea

Krishna R.

Western Ghats

Mangalore •

Bangalore •

Eastern Ghats

• MADRAS

Mysore •

SRI LANKA

Indian Ocean

0   300   600   km

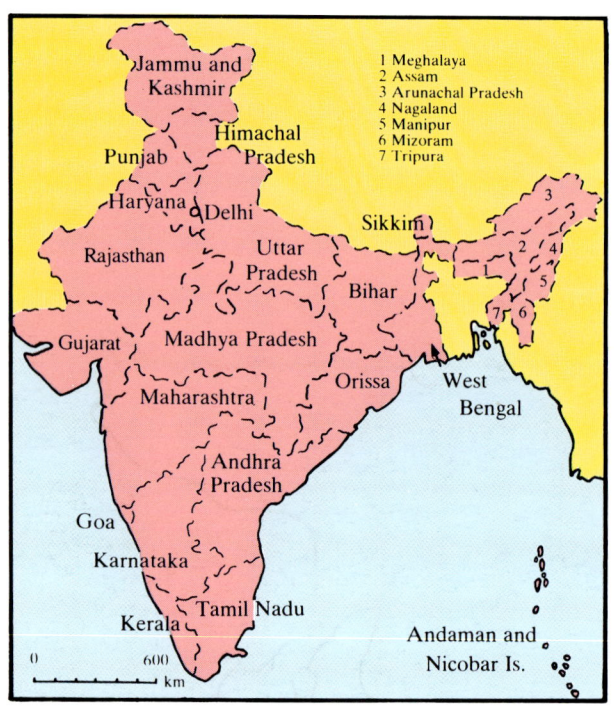

Above *The states and territories of India.*

Indian Ocean and the Bay of Bengal. The principal ports are Bombay in the west and Madras and Calcutta in the east. This diamond-shaped land is divided by the Vindhya mountains, so that the northern regions of the Punjab, Rajasthan, and the fertile plain of the river Ganges, are separated from the Deccan and south India.

The northern plains are hot and dusty in summer but very cold in winter; the Deccan and the south are tropical in character. Although many great rivers and man-made irrigation systems provide water for

Below *The famous Gateway of India in Bombay, the major port on the western coast.*

The Tunga Bhadra Dam at Hampi, in Karnataka. There are many such dams which provide irrigation for large areas of India.

agriculture, large areas still have to depend on the Monsoon rains, which sometimes fail to bring sufficient water to meet the needs of Indian farmers.

India is the most industrialized country in South Asia and tenth among the industrial nations of the world, yet because of its vast, increasing population, rising food production cannot keep pace with poverty and hunger. At present India produces enough food grain to feed the people, but if the Monsoons fail the shortage of basic grain, such as rice, is felt very quickly. In spite of an improvement in wages over the past thirty years, most people are poor and this affects their daily diet which consists of *chapati*-bread, rice and vegetables but lacks proteins and minerals. There is widespread malnutrition in India.

The country produces a variety of grain, oilseed, fruit and vegetables, influencing the eating habits of its people. The climate determines the food grown in the various regions and diet influences the health and stature of the Indian people.

It is impossible to describe the wide variety of food eaten in the whole country in a book of this size, so a selection is presented dealing with as many regions as possible.

Climate and agriculture

The Great Plain of North India is covered with alluvial soils deposited by the river systems of the Indus, the Ganges and the Brahmaputra. This soil is also found in the coastal plains, and it is suitable for growing rice, wheat, corn, sugarcane and oilseeds.

Black soil is most common in central India and the north Deccan. This type of soil retains moisture well and is reasonably fertile, giving good yields of cotton, food grains and oilseeds. Red soils occur in the remaining area of peninsular India; rain-fed crops, such as *jowar* millet, are most suited to this type of soil.

A humid, sub-tropical type of climate is characteristic of the largest area of India. A tropical,

Crushing mustard seed to obtain oil, near Hyderabad, in southern India.

rainy climate is found on the west coast – around Konkan and Kerala – and the north-eastern regions of Bengal and Assam. A desert climate covers a large part of the north western regions of Gujarat and Rajasthan.

Very high rainfall occurs on the west coast and in the north-east, while a large area stretching vertically down the middle of the country has only moderate rainfall. In contrast, the north-western regions of India experience very low levels of rainfall.

The northern plains and the comparatively level areas of the peninsular plateau, forming about 44 per cent of the total area, are cultivated. There are two annual harvests; one in winter, the other in summer. Large areas of the north are irrigated by canals from river dams such as Nangal, Nanaksagar, the Damodar Valley and Hirakud. Similar projects supplement the scanty rainfall in peninsular India. These new irrigation systems have made a major contribution to increasing food production. In many areas water is supplied by wells, using the traditional method of raising water in a large leather bag with the help of bullocks. Complex and simple technologies are thus successfully combined by Indian farmers.

Just under 75 per cent of the Indian population depends on agriculture for its living, and over 40 per cent of the national income is derived from it.

Large-scale farming has been successful in Himachal Pradesh, Punjab and Haryana, where rainfall is low but irrigation is well-developed. Most agricultural land is farmed as 'small-holdings': sons inherit their father's land, so that each field is divided into small strips according to the number of sons. This makes irrigation difficult, as well as fertilization and cultivation of crop-growing areas.

The Government tries to encourage each farmer to own his land, but this leads to uneconomic small farms. Most farmers still use bullock-drawn ploughs. Only in areas of the Punjab and Haryana are tractors readily found, as families in these states have relations working abroad who send money home. Farm-labourers are paid less than factory workers, so many families send one son to work in a factory so that his wages will

Ploughing with tractor and bullock: simple and complex technologies are successfully combined for greater efficiency.

provide ready cash for the family working the village land.

The main food grains produced in India are, in order of importance: rice, wheat, millets like *jowar* and *bajra*, and maize. The maps show major areas of production for grains and pulses.

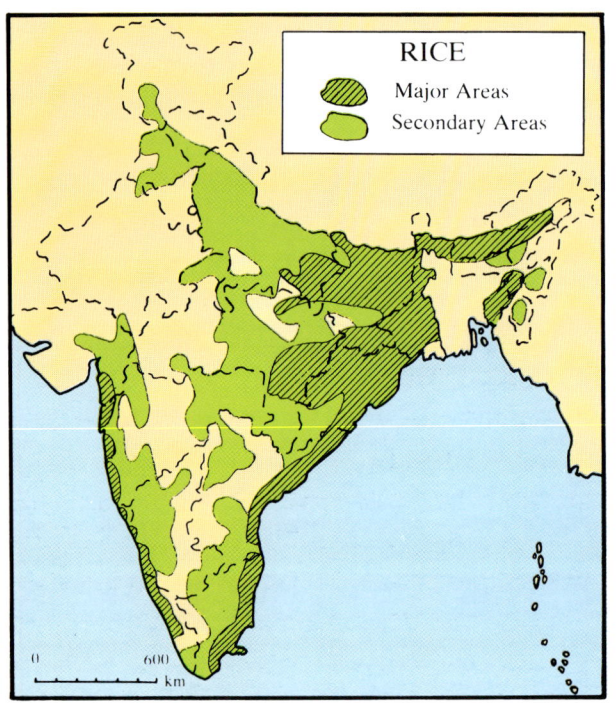

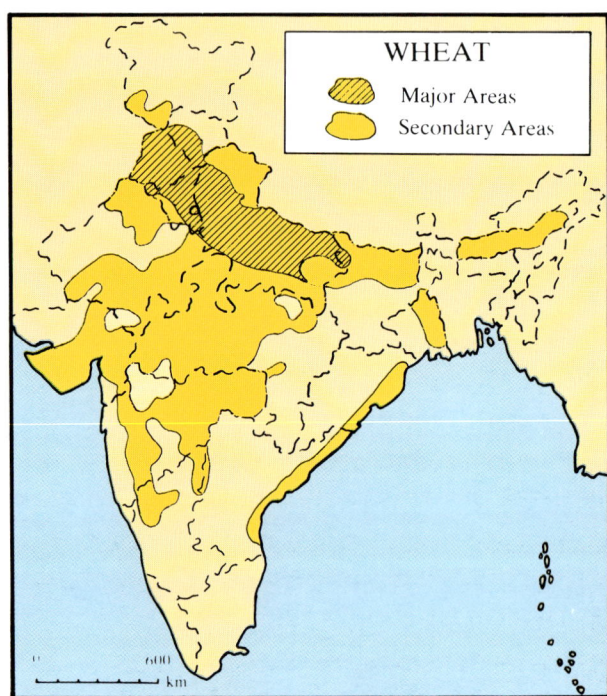

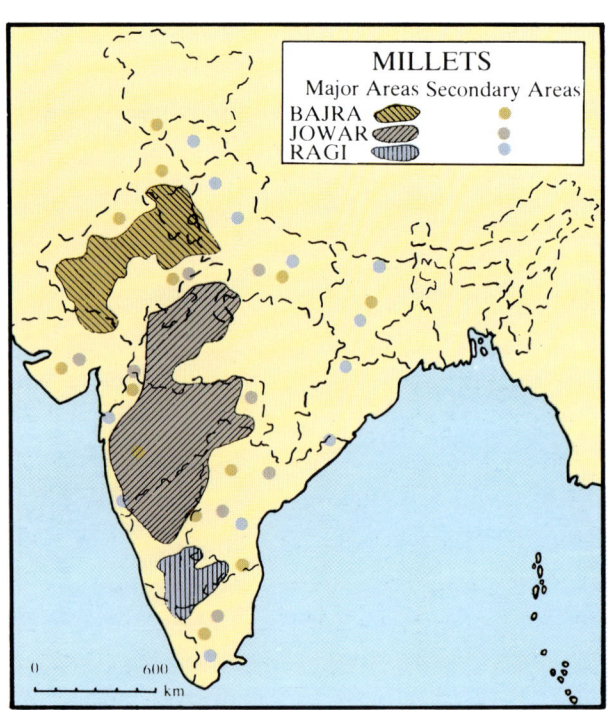

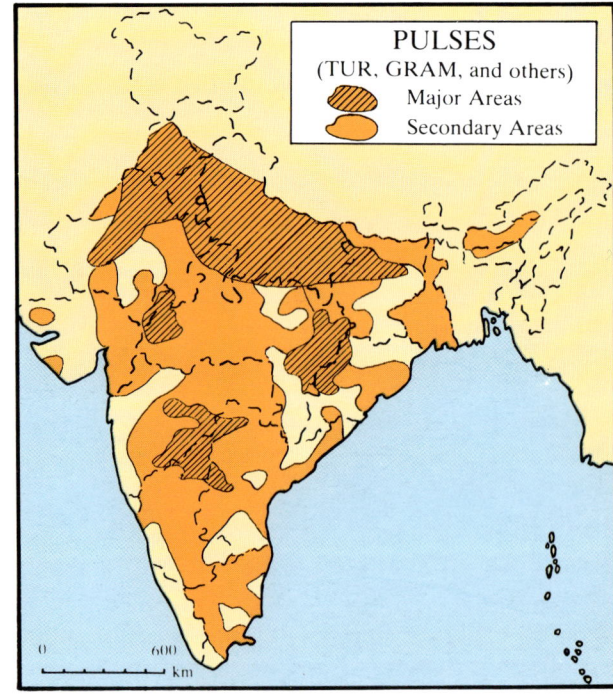

Processing and distribution

After harvesting, the grain (whether rice, wheat, maize, barley or *jowar* millet) is transported by coastal steamers, trains, long distance trucks or bullock carts to the wholesalers in various cities and market towns. The farmer keeps a year's supply for himself and sells the surplus for cash. The wholesaler then distributes the grain to retail shops, where the customer buys it.

Some wheat flour is converted into bread and biscuits by city bakeries, but most people buy the grain and convert it into flour either at the village flour mill or by using a grindstone at home. Most families eat *chapatis*, *parathas* or *purees* (types of unleavened bread) every day, home made from freshly-ground wheat flour, in addition to ready-baked bread which is easily obtained in large cities and towns. In the villages, however, wheat, maize or millet flour is used to make unleavened bread for the day's main meal.

Tea is distributed to towns and villages throughout India from various regional centres. A tea plantation has thousands of bushes and the many workers are trained to pick the tender leaves which are then collected in baskets and carried to large warehouses. The leaves are dried and packed in chests for export: Indian tea reaches all continents of the world.

Half of India's tea is grown in Assam, and about 400,000 men and women work in this industry in Assam alone. The tea industry in India was developed by the British in the 1830s. From the very beginning, tea was grown for export to Britain. At present, India is the leading producer and exporter of tea in the world and tea earns the country valuable income.

For the first hundred years or so, tea workers were poorly paid and at the mercy of the planters. Their lives were so hard that many became addicted to drink or opium. Since the 1940s there has been a slow but gradual improvement in wages, living and working conditions. Medical facilities and

Grain being loaded onto a river barge for transportation to wholesalers.

Tea-pickers on a plantation in Darjeeling.

education were introduced at about the same time. Many tea workers now earn sufficient wages to provide a reasonable living style. The tea industry is one area of work where women often earn more than men because their slim fingers pick the leaves more quickly.

Items such as tea, coffee, bread, biscuits, chocolates, cheese, butter and milk are all bought prepacked. Other foods such as grain, pulses, sugar, cooking oil, fruit and vegetables are sold loose; the customers have to bring their own containers when buying these items. Whisky and beer are, of course, bottled; so are jams, fruit preserves and pickles. *Papadoms* are sold in sealed plastic packets. Ice-cream in paper cups is sold in city shops with deep freezers, but other prepared foods, such as milk sweets, are freshly made and sold within a day.

Crushing sugarcane at a factory. Just one of the many steps in processing the raw material before it reaches the consumer as sugar.

Selling the food

Fruit and vegetable markets are landmarks in every Indian city and town. Business opens at four in the morning and the rush of buyers lasts up to midday. Apples, bananas, oranges, lemons and water melons are available all the year round, while papayas, mangoes, grapes, pears and berries are seasonal. Cabbages, capsicums, cauliflowers, potatoes, onions, tomatoes, carrots, peas, sweet-potatoes and leafy vegetables similar to spinach and watercress are sold in large quantities. Vegetables found in India, but not commonly grown in the West, are ladiesfingers, white gourds, gowar beans, tinders, long white radishes, red pumpkins and purple *brinjals*.

Many barrow-boys sell fruit and vegetables from their hand-carts at street corners, and some bring large baskets of them right up to your front door. Mounds of green chillies, fresh ginger and green coriander, along with betel-leaves, garlic and hard-shelled wood apples for making chutney are a common sight in Indian markets.

Grain shops supply wheat, rice, *jowar* or *bajra* millets, various kinds of beans, chickpeas, lentils, split peas, peanuts, maize, sweetcorn, and flattened or puffed rice. Ground coffee, tea, sugar, biscuits, pickles, jams, cooking oil and many

Vegetable-sellers at a floating market in Kashmir, northern India.

other everyday items are bought from grocery stores.

Visiting a spice-shop in an Indian town is a truly unique experience; spices are sold either as powders or whole seeds, and small quantities are wrapped in little paper packets to order. They give cooked food that unique Indian taste and flavour. You can see red chilli powder, black or grey pepper, cloves, cinnamon, nutmeg and mace, mustard, cumin, turmeric, fennel and many other herbs in a colourful array that would take your breath away.

There are small, kiosk-type shops in cities and towns selling milk sweets, dried fruit and nuts, and rich almond and cashew sweets.

13

Side by side with these kiosks and betel-leaf shops are cafés which sell freshly-fried onion or potato fritters and *samosas*, filled with spiced peas and coriander, in addition to the usual tea, coffee and soft drinks.

Hot food stalls serve dry spiced vegetables with *chapatis*; they may be compared to the 'fast-food' shops which abound in most Western countries.

A most unusual refreshing drink that will quench your thirst on a hot

This café offers a variety of drinks and snacks.

day is fresh coconut milk. Coconuts are picked from the palms just before copra begins to form inside and, when cut open, they contain a milky liquid, slightly sweet and very rich in food value. These are easily available in coastal towns and cities like Bombay and Madras.

In New Delhi, Jaipur, Udaipur, Calcutta, Bombay and Madras, there are five-star, air-conditioned hotels which compare with the best anywhere in the world. The Ashoka, Akabar and Oberoi in Delhi, the Rambagh Palace in Jaipur and the Taj Hotel in Bombay are

famous for their good service and mouthwatering food. There are also popular buffet restaurants in Bombay such as the Bristol-Grill and Rangoli, where meat, fish and vegetarian food is available at moderate prices. Indian brandy and whisky are sold in 'permit' bars and good Indian beer is available in wine and beer shops.

Indian tea

You will need:
500 ml (about 1 pint) water
4 teaspoons of tea-leaves
8 teaspoons of sugar
½ cup of milk
1 teaspoon of crushed ginger
crushed seeds from one cardamon

What to do:
Heat the water, tea-leaves, sugar and milk together in a saucepan (1). Add the crushed cardamon seeds and the fresh ginger (2). Remove the pan from the heat as soon as the tea comes to the boil (3). Strain into a teapot ready for serving (4). The drink produced in this way may not be the normal cup of tea most Westerners are used to, but it is very tasty indeed.

Safety note: Be careful, as boiling liquids can be very dangerous and can scald severely. Get an adult to help you strain the tea into the pot.

The midday meal

In India a midday meal in villages and small towns may require about two hours of preparation and cooking. In rural areas, very few people buy ready-baked bread, so they have to prepare *chapatis* or *purees* from wheat flour, or bake unleavened bread from millet or rice flour on an iron bakestone over a wood-burning stove. Some families are lucky enough to have a two-ring cooker using cylinder gas.

Vegetables are bought at the market and need cleaning and washing before they are cooked. The rice grains have to be carefully sorted out to avoid grit. The making of dough, and the rolling or flattening of it by hand is a delicate and complicated skill. The flattened dough has to be transferred to the

Rather than buying ready-ground flour, most people buy the grain themselves and grind it at home, or at the village flour mill.

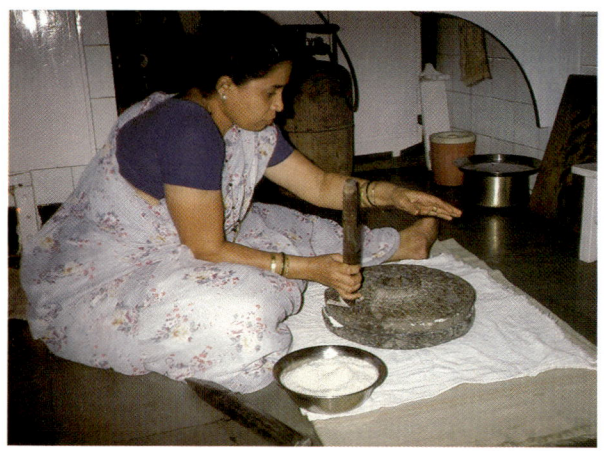

A tiffin carrier in Bombay. Around 500,000 lunches are delivered by tiffin carriers each day.

hot bakestone and needs constant attention since a wood fire cannot be controlled as easily as a gas stove. The vegetables are usually spiced and turned into a light stew or curry. There may be freshly ground chilli and green coriander chutney at the midday meal. The rice is normally boiled in lightly-salted water.

In large cities, where incomes are higher, people at work can get a hot meal at a food stall, a café, an office canteen or at an expensive restaurant. Those women who do not have jobs usually eat their midday meal at home, just as elderly people and schoolchildren do. Sometimes *chapati*-making is done by women who visit other people's houses during the

Washing-up after the midday meal.

morning and prepare *chapatis* for the whole family. They may visit as many as ten houses each day, earning a fair living. In urban homes, rice and other dishes can be prepared fairly easily, since most families will possess a gas stove.

Many office workers in Bombay have their lunch sent to them by 'tiffin-carrier'. A large number of men earn their living by this 'meals-on-wheels' service, which transports around half-a-million lunches from the suburbs to the main business area each day, using taxis, bicycles, trains and push-carts. It is truly a remarkable operation and rarely does a tiffin-carrier fail to reach his destination.

Indians do not drink tea or coffee immediately after their midday meal, as many Westerners do. They may, however, have some fruit juice or buttermilk with their lunch. In India the water buffalo, not the cow, is the main source of milk. Most people drink a lot of water, not only at meal times but also throughout the day, to keep their bodies cool.

Recipes for a complete midday meal

These items can be prepared easily in a cookery class, or at home with the help of a parent. The spices can be obtained from any supermarket. Together, the four items will make a good lunch for four people.

Tomato and onion chutney

You will need:
2 small tomatoes
2 small onions
1 teaspoon of sugar
cayenne pepper
natural yoghurt
salt

What to do:
Chop the onions and tomatoes finely. Add one teaspoon of sugar and half a teaspoon of salt and pepper. Add five tablespoons of natural yoghurt. Stir the mixture well. Put the chutney into the fridge to chill before serving.

Purees

You will need:
4 cups of wholemeal flour
at least 1 large cup of vegetable oil
a little water
salt

What to do:
Prepare the dough using flour, a little water, one teaspoonful of oil and a pinch of salt. Knead the dough well. Make balls the size of a small tomato. Roll the balls into flat discs about 8 cm (3 in) across. Pour a large cupful of oil into a deep frying pan. Fry each disc, turning it over until puffed and browned. Carefully remove hot *purees* into a large dish. They are now ready to serve.

Masala rice

You will need:

240 g (about 8 oz) Basmati rice
120 g (4 oz) frozen peas
60 g (2 oz) cashew nuts or salted
   peanuts
1 large onion
½ teaspoon of turmeric
pinch of cumin seeds
8 cloves
small stick of cinnamon
1 tablespoon of butter
salt

What to do:

Wash and cook the rice (see instructions on page 30) so that the grains are separated. Heat the butter in another saucepan and add the cumin seeds, turmeric, cloves, cinnamon and salt (1). Finely chop the onion (2). Add the onion, peas and nuts and fry on a low heat, keeping the lid on the saucepan (3). When the onions are brown, add the cooked rice and stir well (4). Remove from heat and serve (5).

Safety note: When frying, be careful not to get the butter in the pan too hot, as it can be very dangerous.

Lamb curry

You will need:

240 g (about 8 oz) chopped and boned
   lamb
1 large onion
2 potatoes
small tin of peeled tomatoes
½ teaspoon of turmeric
pinch of mustard seeds
1 teaspoon of garam masala
1 teaspoon of coriander powder
1 tablespoon of vegetable oil
salt

What to do:

Peel and chop the potatoes (1). Heat the
oil in a saucepan. Add the mustard seeds
and put the lid on when they start to 'pop'
(2). Then add the turmeric, garam masala,
coriander, chopped onion and a little salt
(3). Fry the mixture until the onion is
brown (4). Add the lamb pieces, tomatoes
and potatoes (5). Cook on a low heat until
the meat is tender.

Safety note: Be very careful with sharp
knives when chopping vegetables,
especially tough ones like potatoes. Ask
an adult to help.

2

3

4

1

5

Regional foods: the north

Punjab

Sikhism was founded about 500 years ago in the Punjab by the first of the ten Sikh *gurus*, or teachers, Guru Nanak. The religion owes something to both Hinduism and Islam, and a strongly-united brotherhood of Sikhs, the *Khalsa* (pure ones), was established by Guru Gobind Singh in the seventeenth century. In India as a whole, Sikhs are a small minority (only 1.9 per cent) but they are concentrated in the Punjab, where they slightly outnumber Hindus. There are no images in Sikh temples (*Gurudwara*) and the food found there is vegetarian, as the temples are open to visitors of all faiths. Most Sikhs eat meat themselves, with the exception of beef that is.

It is difficult to distinguish between the regional foods of northern India, because many

A selection of unleavened breads: paratha *(bottom right),* tandoori roti *(top right),* nan *(bottom left),* chapati *(middle left) and* purees *(top left).*

Potato, tomato and ginger savoury

You will need:
480 g (about 1 lb) potatoes
1½ cm (about ½ in) stem ginger
120 g (4 oz) firm, ripe tomatoes
1 tablespoon of vegetable oil
1 cupful of water
cumin seeds
mustard seeds
turmeric
garam masala
chilli powder
salt

What to do:
Peel and chop the potatoes, chop the tomatoes and grate the ginger (1). Heat the oil in a saucepan and drop in the cumin and mustard seeds. Cover the pan while the seeds 'pop' (2). Add the grated ginger and a pinch of turmeric, garam masala, chilli powder and salt. Stir well (3). Add the chopped tomatoes and cover the pan. After 3 minutes add the water and potatoes (4). Cook on a low heat until the potatoes are soft, being careful not to let the mixture dry out and burn. Add more water if necessary to prevent this.

Safety note: Always be careful when using chilli powder, hot pepper or curry powder. Use in small quantities and keep away from your eyes.

dishes are common to the whole area. In wheat-growing Punjab and Haryana the main meal rarely begins without thick *parathas*, cooked first on bakestones and then flat-fried in oil. Lentils cooked with fried mustard seeds, turmeric and garlic are delicious with the crisp *parathas*.

Potatoes cooked with ginger, cumin seed and turmeric, in a sauce of fresh chopped tomatoes, can be prepared without much difficulty and served as a vegetable dish (see recipe). Orthodox Hindus do not eat meat, but people of other religions often eat lamb curry with their *parathas*. A simple ready-spiced salad can be made with sliced tomatoes, onion and cucumber sprinkled with a little salt and chilli powder.

Delhi, Uttar Pradesh and Bihar

Delhi has been India's capital city for the last eight hundred years, and successive rulers of India have left behind their own particular styles of cooking, which later generations have adapted. The results are always tempting. In expensive hotels, as well as hot

A buffet in Delhi's Oberoi Hotel. Delhi, like other large Indian cities, has hotels which compare with the best anywhere in the world.

food stalls by the roadside, one can find lamb fillets flat-fried, with the addition of garlic and capsicums. The traditional British lamb chop has been transformed and turned into a delicious Indian dish.

Delhi and north-Indian cooking has a great deal of Mogul influence and modern dishes do not vary much from the original.

A rice dish called *pullao* is made from boiled rice mixed with spices and small pieces of cauliflower or garden peas. *Pullao* tastes different in other regions because the method of preparation and the spices used are different. Ordinary split peas are cooked with oil and cumin seeds and brought to life with green coriander. Lamb is cooked with spinach and onions, black pepper and cardamons. Vegetarians prepare dishes of ladiesfingers stuffed with coriander, and chickpea-flour dumplings in a thick sauce. *Purees* are small circles of rolled wheat-flour dough, deep fried in oil until they are brown; they puff up like balloons.

A characteristic of cooking in the Hindu city of Varanasi, in Uttar Pradesh, is that it excludes onions and garlic. Meals are served on metal plates (*thalis*) directly from the cooking pots, so as to maintain the distinct tastes of the dishes. In Varanasi, high quality milk products such as sweet, spiced *shrikhand* and buttermilk spiced with cumin seeds and fresh loaves of

Tandoori *chicken, a favourite dish in Uttar Pradesh, is spiced and cooked in a clay oven.*

green coriander are the city's specialities.

In contrast to Varanasi, Lucknow – also in Uttar Pradesh – is a Muslim city. Muslims do not eat pork and (in India) rarely eat beef; their meat is usually lamb, goat or chicken. In Lucknow one could drown in rich food at formal dinners! Legs of lamb cooked with almonds, kebabs (pieces of lamb) cooked with cumin and fennel seeds, rice and meat broth, natural yoghurt and chutney are all served with great hospitality.

Dry vegetable curry made with spiced cauliflower is also popular. Beefburger-shaped lamb kebabs are sold at hot food stalls in Lucknow and *tandoori* chicken is spiced and cooked in a clay oven — a *tandoor*.

In Rajasthan, west of Uttar Pradesh, and in Madhya Pradesh, a rich dish is prepared using chicken marinated with saffron, and spiced with cinnamon, cloves, cardamon and coriander seeds.

Indian beer, brewed in the northern parts of Uttar Pradesh, is of good quality and fairly inexpensive. Friends will sometimes go to a bar together to drink beer, but no women are ever seen in these bars. A beer bar in India is not a social meeting place in the way that bars or pubs are in Western countries. Beer or wine in these bars is more expensive than that sold in shops. For Muslims alcohol is forbidden by their religion and it is not favoured by Hinduism or Sikhism, though many Hindus and Sikhs do drink beer and spirits.

Freshwater fish, especially carp, are popular in Bengal. They are often served in a spicy sauce with boiled rice.

Bengal

The state of West Bengal is long and narrow, running from the mouths of the River Ganges at the Bay of Bengal in the south to the heights of the Himalayas at Darjeeling in the north. People living in Bengal are very fond of freshwater fish, delicately spiced in a thick sauce and served with plain boiled rice. Bengalis do eat meat, in the form of chicken or lamb curries, but they prefer fish to any other type of non-vegetarian food.

Carp, eaten with rice, is a favourite Bengali dish. Sometimes the carp is cooked in a thin sauce of cumin and coriander seeds, turmeric and red chillies. Chillies,

either whole or in powdered form, are very pungent and can be dangerous to your eyes, mouth and stomach. They should be used in very small quantities and only by those who know how to use them. Another typical dish from Calcutta, the capital of Bengal, is prawn curry seasoned with mustard seeds.

Vegetable curry made with white radishes and potatoes is a popular lunchtime dish. This meal will probably include some vegetable fritters, lightly spiced and fried in groundnut oil. Cereals such as *moong* are spiced while cooking and served as a side dish. Vegetables such as ladiesfingers and red pumpkin are also popular, along with cauliflowers, potatoes, and many kinds of spinach. Tomatoes are the main ingredient of most sweet or sour chutneys.

A colourful array of red and green chillis. Chillis are used extensively throughout India.

Puffed rice in full-cream milk mixed with mango slices or bananas, is a commonly enjoyed sweet dish. Milk sweets are an essential part of a meal in Bengal; indeed, they are popular throughout northern and western India.

Gujarat

This new state was formed in 1960 and lies to the north of India's western coast. Gujarati food is available wherever Gujarati-speaking people have migrated, whether to East Africa or Britain. People belonging to three different religions speak Gujarati, and as a result a variety of foods are eaten by these people.

Firstly, the Hindus are mainly vegetarian; they eat rice, spiced vegetables, pulses, *purees, dhokala* (a preparation made from chickpea flour spiced with garlic), a variety of milk sweets such as *kheer* (a spiced rice or crushed wheat pudding) *basundi* and many varieties of *halva* made from milk and dried fruits. Generally speaking, Gujarati Hindus use plenty of peanut oil, red chilli powder and garlic in their savoury curries and soups.

Secondly, the Boharas are Gujarati-speaking Muslims who eat meat along with many other common dishes. They prepare a special dish for wedding feasts, using flaky pastry and clotted cream. Bohara soups are made from *toor-dal*, chopped cucumber and tomatoes.

The third Gujarati-speaking group are the Parsis, whose ancestors left Iran in the eighth century AD and settled on the west coast of India. A large number of Parsis live in Bombay and the best Parsi food is usually found at wedding feasts. There will be delicately spiced chicken, spiced vegetable mixtures of potatoes, spinach and tomatoes, sweet corn cooked with cumin and green

Halva, *made from milk and dried nuts or fruit, is one of many varieties of milk sweet popular with Gujarati Hindus.*

coriander, *chapatis*, and steamed fish with *dhanya* chutney.

Another typical snack from Gujarat is the triangular *samosa*, stuffed with potatoes and assorted vegetables, spiced with chilli powder and garlic and deep fried in groundnut oil.

Chapatis

You will need (to make 6 chapatis):
2 cups of wholemeal flour
3 teaspoons of vegetable oil
½ cup of water
a pinch of salt
butter

What to do:
Mix the flour, vegetable oil and salt in a mixing bowl. Add water gradually to prepare a thick dough (1). Knead the dough well. Divide the dough into 6 equal portions (2). Flatten each portion with a rolling pin. Try to roll out a circle of dough about 3 mm (¹⁄₁₀ in) thick and 12 cm (5 in) across (3). Heat a frying pan on a low flame, cook the *chapati* evenly, turning over to avoid burning (4). As it cooks, it will puff up. Place the hot *chapati* on a plate and spread with *ghee* or butter before serving.

Safety note: Be careful transferring the *chapati* (or any other hot foods) from the pan to a plate. Use a long flat spatula or slice to do this.

The evening meal

Food habits are determined by many things such as availability of foodstuffs, climate and religion. Generally speaking, city dwellers who rush about all day making a living tend to have a small lunch and a large evening meal. People who live in the country, on the other hand, have a large midday meal and eat little in the evening.

A well-paid civil servant in New Delhi is more likely to have a few guests for a large evening meal than at lunch. Such a meal would include meat or chicken curry with *parathas* and mixed spiced vegetables. There would be vegetable *pullao* to follow. The side dishes would include *papadoms*, well-fried in oil and yoghurt chutney with finely chopped tomatoes, onions, and red chilli powder. Specially-bought ice-cream would be served with coffee and dried fruit and nuts. Guests would receive

A betel-leaf seller. The leaves, very hot when chewed, are used as a digestive aid.

29

A light evening meal, preceded by prayers, in an urban home.

betel-leaves, spices and betel-nuts as digestive aids.

A Bombay bank official or a junior executive could be a vegetarian and enjoy a meal which includes his favourite dishes: steamed rice topped with thick lentil soup (*dal*) and *ghee* would be the first course. Hot pickles and roasted *papadoms* would add a sharp taste to the fried spinach, potato *bhajee* and churned-yoghurt curry spiced with *kadhi-limba* (sweet leaves) and cumin seeds. A few coriander fritters would be relished with *jowar*-millet griddle bread. The last course would be rice and natural yoghurt with a pinch of salt. The spicing in this Bombay meal would be delicately done so as not to drown the natural taste and flavour of the vegetables.

In Gujarat, the evening meal would be mainly rice with vegetable curry, prepared with plenty of oil, spices and chilli powder. *Dhokala*, made from chickpea flour, would be a side dish. The last course would be steamed rice eaten with milk. Milk sweets such as *halva* or *burfee* are served after dinner.

In towns and villages, millet bread served with spiced pulses or some vegetable curry would suffice for an evening meal. In southern India rice dishes tend to dominate every meal.

Recipes for a complete evening meal

The spices used in these recipes can be obtained from any supermarket. The items listed here will make a light evening meal for three people.

Boiled rice

You will need:
240 g (about 8 oz) Basmati rice
2 cups of water
pinch of salt

What to do:
Wash the rice. Add the rice to boiling, salted water. Cook the rice for about 15 minutes, or until the grains are soft. Drain the rice and serve.

Safety note: When testing to see that the rice is cooked, ask an adult to scoop out a few grains. Wait for the grains to cool and then taste them. Ask an adult to help you drain the rice with a colander or a sieve.

Spinach *dal*

You will need:
240 g (about 8 oz) lentils
tin of chopped spinach
60 g (2 oz) natural peanuts
1 tablespoon of vegetable oil
mustard seeds
turmeric
curry powder
salt

What to do:
Wash and cook the lentils separately (1). Heat the oil in a large saucepan. Add a few mustard seeds and put the lid on the saucepan when they begin to 'pop' (2). Add turmeric, salt and curry powder in small quantities. Carefully add the chopped spinach, peanuts and a little water (3). Boil the spinach and spices for 5 minutes, then add the lentils and stir well (4). Simmer the spinach *dal* on a low heat for about 20 minutes, when it will be ready to serve (5).

Safety note: Always be very careful when opening a tin of food — the edges of an opened tin are jagged and very sharp. Frozen spinach can be used as an alternative.

Onion fritters

You will need:
1 cup of chickpea flour
1 cup of vegetable oil
2 small onions
a little water
salt

What to do:
Chop the onions finely. Gradually mix the flour, onion, salt and water to make a liquid of medium thickness. Heat the oil in a deep frying pan and add the flour liquid one tablespoonful at a time. Each spoonful forms a crispy fritter. Fry well and carefully remove fritters to a dish.

Cucumber chutney

You will need:
120 g (about 4 oz) salted peanuts
4 tablespoons of natural yoghurt
1 small cucumber
1 tablespoon of vegetable oil
cumin seeds, turmeric and salt
cayenne pepper
sugar

What to do:
Slice the cucumber finely and crush the peanuts (1). Mix the two together. Add a little salt, sugar and pepper. Heat the oil in a small saucepan and add a pinch of cumin seeds and turmeric (2). Pour the oil and spices into the cucumber mixture (3). Then add the natural yoghurt and stir well (4).

Regional foods: the south

Tamil Nadu and Karnataka

Most of southern India is a vast rice growing region, and vegetarian food in Karnataka and Tamil Nadu consists of many variations on the basic theme of rice. Although chicken is enjoyed by many in cities like Madras, Bangalore and Mysore, the main food is rice and fresh vegetables.

Rice grains, simply boiled, may appear to us to be a poor meal, but different processes like grinding, pounding, steaming and frying transform rice and other cereals into tasty dishes. A simple meal in Madras consists of rice and a hot thin soup called *rasam*, followed by more rice and *rasam*, and finally by rice, yoghurt and hot pickles. Since rice is to a south Indian what potatoes are to the Western

Much of southern India is a vast rice-growing region. Below, livestock are used to plough irrigated paddy fields.

European, it is not surprising that large quantities are eaten at a single meal.

We have seen wheat flour turned into *chapatis* or *purees*. In the south, rice and *urad-dal* flour are made into *doshé* (pancakes) which are served with pickles or spiced vegetables. When served at lunchtime, this can form the middle course.

A variety of vegetable dishes are available, but cucumber salad, cauliflower with red chillies and *sambar* are very popular. *Sambar* is a

Sambar *and* idali, *two favourite Tamil foods.*

hot, soup-like preparation made from a mixture of *toor-dal* powder, spices and water. There are variations in taste when different cereals are used.

On the west coast near Mangalore many varieties of fish are available and small fish like mackerel are seasoned with tamarind, garlic and chillies and served fried.

A typical Tamil food is *idali*. It resembles the white part of a poached egg and is made with a stone-ground mixture of rice and *urad-dal*. The dough is poured into moulds in a metal plate and steamed. *Idali* and *Sambar* are also enjoyed in non-Tamil cities like Bombay by Maharashtrans, who normally use *urad-dal* flour for making *papadoms*.

Maharashtra

Maharashtra is a hilly and rugged area of western India. In this region three different styles of cooking exist and they depend very much on social status as well as family traditions.

Historically, Hindu society has been divided up into hundreds of different classes, or 'castes', based on the kind of work people used to do. The *Brahmins* were teachers, priests, doctors and so on. There were also castes of soldiers, rulers and princes, called *Kshatriyas*. *Vaishya* castes were merchants, shopkeepers and farmers, while

Shudras were workers such as basket-weavers, black-smiths and farm labourers. Leather-workers or those who swept the streets and cleared the rubbish were 'untouchables' or *Harijans*. They were the poorest caste of all and badly treated, but untouchability is now illegal in modern India. The caste system affects people's eating habits also. For instance, *Vaishyas* are usually vegetarian, but *Kshatriyas* and *Shudras* eat meat though not beef.

Spices are an essential part of Indian cooking and give it its own particular flavour. They are generally sold loose, at spice shops like the one shown below.

The Hindu *Brahmins*, of whom there are many in Maharashtra, are also vegetarians. Like other people of this region, they eat wheat as well as rice. Generally speaking, people to the north of Maharashtra will eat wheat or maize, while those to the south favour rice. In Bombay, Poona, Satara or Kolhapur one finds rice and wheat along with millets like *jowar* or *bajra* used in a variety of ways. *Brahmin* cooking is delicately spiced with chillies (never too hot) and designed to bring out the flavour of each ingredient.

Griddle breads of millet flour, or *chapatis* made from wheat flour, along with steamed or spiced rice

appear at every meal. Other regular favourites are spiced vegetables like gowar beans, spinach with potatoes, cauliflower with carrots, soaked pulses and beans, white gourds or snake-gourds, pumpkins, and sweet potatoes. These are washed down with tomato soup (*sar*) or thin curries made with *toor-dal*, lentils or chickpeas. Special salads of grated cucumber, peanuts and green tomatoes spiced with cumin seeds are unique to this region. Rice-flour pancakes, potato

A Maharashtran woman selects small fish to be salted and dried.

filled *wada*, or a savoury flattened rice mixture (*chivada*) serve as snacks.

Beyond the mountains known as the Western Ghats, the farmers enjoy meat curries cooked in Kolhapuri style, using oil and red chillies liberally. They do not care much for the rice and milk sweets of the *Brahmins*, but enjoy their staple bread of *jowar* or *bajra* millet with black beans, carrots or onions hot with chillies.

Between the mountain range and the Arabian sea lies the narrow strip of Konkan where the Koli fishermen bring in hauls of sea pomfret and mackerel. Small fish like sardines are salted and dried. When they are fried they taste delicious, but the smell is enough to make the neighbours emigrate beyond the Western Ghats!

Kerala

Kerala is a narrow, fertile strip of land on the south-west coast of India, bordered by the Western Ghats. In this state Hindus, Muslims, Jews and Christians live in harmony and enjoy the tropical bounty of fish, fruit, coconuts and vegetables. Important spices like pepper, nutmeg, cloves, cinnamon and turmeric are grown in Kerala in abundance and these spices, especially black pepper, brought foreign traders to Kerala in the past.

Vegetarian Hindus serve rice with a mixture of vegetables

Coconuts drying in the sun. Coconut is an important ingredient in many Keralan dishes.

including carrots, beans and spinach spiced with *kadhi-limba* leaves and fresh coconut. Rice and coconut make their appearance with unfailing regularity. Fresh coconut is an important ingredient in many vegetable curries.

Curried prawns spiced with *dhanya* seeds and fresh tamarind, and thinned with coconut milk, is another local dish that goes well with steamed rice. Chicken cooked with green chillies is particularly relished by Kerala's Jewish community, who prefer to eat it with rice.

A mixture of finely chopped green vegetables and fruit is mixed with natural yoghurt and spiced with cumin seeds fried in coconut oil. This is served with almost any type of food in Kerala.

Special foods

Festive Food

There are many annual religious festivals in India. The most important for Muslims are the *Id* festivals, for Sikhs *Baishakhi* and the birthday of Guru Nanak, for Christians Christmas and Easter, and for Hindus *Diwali, Navaratri, Holi* and the Ganesha festival. Ritual celebrations are varied but, as with religious festivals everywhere, the preparation and serving of special, delicious foods is an important part of the enjoyment.

Although traditional meat and poultry dishes are served at the festivals of minority religions like Islam and Christianity, only vegetarian food is prepared on Hindu festival days. It is impossible to give all the regional variations, but at many public festivals a special sweet dish is offered to the

Hindu festivals are always colourful. The preparation and serving of special food is often a vital part of the occasion.

deity, received back as a blessed offering, and distributed to all the worshippers present. A large quantity of semolina is heated in a big pan with *ghee*, until the semolina is quite brown. Crushed cardamon seeds are then added and the mixture is cooked in milk. The result is a solid pudding, to which are added sliced bananas. This *halva*, or *shira*, is a very popular festival food.

Not all Hindu festivals are celebrated by public worship in a temple. Some are, in fact, home-based festive occasions when particular sweet dishes are prepared. Two such dishes are described below because they are unusual.

In Gujarat and western India, on the *Devi* festival days, stuffed *chapatis – puran polees –* are enjoyed by many families. Self-raising flour dough is rolled out in a circular disc about 8 cm (3 in) across, into which a spoonful of cooked chickpea and jaggary mixture is enclosed to form a ball. It is then rolled out into a chapati about seven inches across, and cooked on a flat bakestone. This deliciously crumbly and flaky chapati is then served with lashings of *ghee* or milk.

On the Ganesha festival day in Maharashtra a rice-flour dumpling called *modak* is always prepared at home. Rice flour is mixed with water and lightly cooked. This dough is then flattened into small discs by hand and previously-

Preparing modak: *the coconut and jaggary mixture is enclosed within a cone of dough and steamed for about twenty minutes.*

cooked coconut and jaggary stuffing is enclosed to form a cone with corrugated sides. These dumplings are then steamed for about twenty minutes and served, hot or cold, with *ghee*. To prepare the rice flour, the grains are soaked in water and partly dried overnight, before they are stone-ground at home to obtain flour with the right texture. Flour made from dry rice grains becomes too fine and does not produce a suitable dough.

Wedding feasts

Indian marriages are more than the uniting of a bride and groom; they also join together families, and the new relationship formed between these groups is celebrated by a rich and joyful meal. This is true for Hindus, Muslims, Christians and Sikhs, the only differences being the types of food served at the marriage feasts. At Hindu weddings in India vegetarian food is served, for guests from various social groups may be present, and none should be offended by the food served. Muslims, Christians and Sikhs may serve meat dishes, but the special sweets described here are served by all religious groups.

Weddings are religious as well as social occasions and the main sweet dish at the wedding feast can either make or spoil the day. Although it is called a 'sweet', it is in fact the main dish, served as a middle course until all the guests have been coaxed into over-eating! By and large there are three favourites: *ladoos*, *jilebees* and *shrikhand*.

A thin dough of semolina is spread onto a large iron sieve with a handle and small globules of it are thrown into very hot *ghee*. They are fried instantly, and quickly collected and poured into a large brass serving dish. Granulated sugar is mixed with these *bundis*, as they are called, and the mixture is made into balls the size of half a tennis ball. Hot *ghee* and sugar bind

Special sweetmeats are served at wedding feasts by all religious groups. The most popular of these sweetmeats are ladoos, jilebees *and* shrikhand.

the globules together firmly and *bundi-ladoos* are ready to be served, usually cold.

Jilebees are also prepared from semolina, the thin dough being squeezed from a mould and dropped into boiling *ghee* so that it emerges like long thin spaghetti. The dough forms a long tube, in the shape of a circular squiggle. When fried until brown, the squiggles are dipped into syrup flavoured with saffron and yellowed with artificial colouring. *Jilebees* are always served cold.

For *shrikhand* a thick layer of natural yoghurt is spread on a clean linen cloth on the ground. The

Semolina dough is squeezed into boiling ghee *to make* jilebees.

moisture soon disappears into the ground and a thick substance like cream cheese is left behind. Crushed cardamon, heated saffron and chopped white almonds and sugar are then added and the mixture is thoroughly stirred. The sugar gradually dissolves and a highly spiced yoghurt – *shrikhand* – is ready to serve. *Shrikhand* is normally eaten with *purees*.

There are, of course, other regional variations but these three dishes are eaten throughout India.

Indian food in other countries

Indian people have travelled throughout the world and settled in South-East Asia, East and South Africa, the West Indies, Mauritius, Fiji and Canada for many generations. More recently, they have also moved to Britain, the USA and Australia. Wherever they have gone, they have taken their food habits with them and have made use of locally grown vegetables and grains to make a wide variety of dishes. The spices that are needed are widely available and such dairy products as milk, butter and yoghurt can be found everywhere. However, Indian food found outside India will not be quite the same, since Indian veget-

Indian Sikh women preparing food at a wedding feast in Britain. There are many Indian communities throughout the world.

ables are not always easy to obtain and alternatives have to be found.

In Britain, Indian food began to be available in the dockland areas of London and other ports in the 1930s, when Indian eating houses were established to cater for the Indian sailors. Indian grocery shops stocked all the spices necessary for Indian cooking, but no Indian vegetables were available since cargo ships took over seven weeks to travel to Britain.

Later air cargo facilities enabled importers to bring in many different items to satisfy the needs of Indian families settled in Britain.

Many cities of the world now have restaurants and takeaway shops. These restaurants provide vegetable, meat and chicken curries differently-spiced according to regional varieties such as Delhi, Bombay or Madras. Prawns and fish are made into mouth watering dishes. Also available are different types of fritters, *samosas, chapatis, nan* stuffed with spiced minced meat, *purees, parathas* and *papadoms*. Chicken, meat or vegetable *biriyanis* are popular rice dishes, each with its own particular flavour.

It is said that variety is the spice of life but these spiced dishes from India have provided the variety that enriches eating habits throughout the world.

An array of Indian foods: a selection of spices (top centre), Chapatis *(top right), chicken and prawn* pullao *(middle left),* dal *(centre),* papadoms *(middle right), dry beef curry (bottom left), mango chutney (bottom centre) and dry chicken curry (bottom right). Although the presentation and ingredients may differ slightly, the unique character and taste of Indian food is the same throughout the world.*

Appendix

Cooking and eating utensils

Some utensils used in the cooking, serving and eating of food in India look slightly unusual to Western eyes, although they are used essentially for the same purposes as more familiar cooking utensils. The table below describes a few of these items. You may be able to recognize them in the photographs.

In parts of India (particularly the south) eating utensils are not used at all. Instead, the food is scooped up with the fingers of the right hand. It is said that eating in this way allows you to get the 'feel' of the food, which is almost as important in south Indian cuisine as the aroma or the presentation is in other styles of cooking.

Tawa (*chapati* pan)	A cast iron circular plate, about 18-20 cm (7–8 in) across, with or without a handle.	
Kadhee	A cast iron bowl with handles, for deep frying.	
Chokla Belma	A circular wooden board and pin for flattening and rolling the *chapati* dough.	
Paraat	A brass or stainless steel shallow mixing bowl for preparing dough.	
Patelaa	A stainless steel cooking pan with lid, with or without a handle.	
Paylaa	A stainless steel drinking cup.	
Serving Set	A three-bowl serving set with one handle for serving different curries and chutneys.	
Thali	A dinner plate of tin-plated brass or stainless steel, about 15 cm (6 in) across.	
Watee, Kauli or *Katori*	Small steel bowls, about 7 or 8 cm (3 in) across for serving different liquid dishes.	

Glossary

Alluvial Alluvial soils are those which have been deposited by the action of rivers.

Bajra The grey millet grown in western India.

Basundi Thickened milk with sugar, saffron and cardamon.

Betel-leaf The leaf of a creeper used as a digestive aid.

Brinjal A small, round variety of aubergine.

Biriyani Spiced rice with cooked meat or chicken.

Bhajee Vegetable curry.

Burfee A milk sweet with nuts.

Caste One of the Hindu hereditary classes, in which members are socially equal, united in religion and historically followed the same trades. Social mixing with other castes was discouraged.

Chapati Unleavened bread made from wheat flour and cooked on a flat iron bakestone.

Chilli A hot spice, available as a red powder or as red or green bean-like fruits.

Chivada A savoury mixture of flattened rice, fried nuts, copra, spices, oil and *khadi-limba*.

Copra The dried kernel of coconut.

Curry A general term used to describe a dish (meat, fish, egg, etc) cooked with crushed spices and turmeric.

Dal Dry, split cereals such as *toor*, *moong* or *masur*, or a thin soup-like curry made from them.

Deccan A flat plain between the Eastern and Western Ghats.

Dhanya Either the seeds or the green leaves of coriander.

Dhokala A preparation made from chickpea flour, spices, oil and garlic.

Doshé A rice-flour pancake.

Garam masala A pungent mixture of various spices.

Ghee Butter which is free from impurities.

Gowar beans Thin, flat green beans.

Halva A solid pudding made from semolina, sugar, milk, butter, cardamon and almonds.

Idali A preparation made from rice and *urad* flour.

Jaggary Raw, unrefined sugar.

Jilebees Circular squiggles made from semolina, *ghee*, syrup, saffron and colouring.

Jowar The great millet grown in central and western India.

Khadi-limba Sweet, fragrant leaves used as flavouring in Indian cooking.

Kebab Minced meat, mildly spiced and roasted on skewers.

Kheer A sweet, similar to rice pudding.

Kurma A very mild curry (meat or chicken) with coconut and cream.

Ladiesfingers Indian green beans.

Ladoos Sweet balls of semolina, sugar and *ghee*.

Modak A rice flour dumpling with cooked, fresh coconut and jaggary stuffing.

Mogul Relating to the Mogul empire of India and its Muslim emperors, who reigned from the sixteenth to the eighteenth centuries.

Monsoons Seasonal heavy rain in the south-western and north-eastern parts of India.

Moong Green gram, an important cereal in south India.

Mysore-paak A sweet made with sugar and chickpea flour, richly fried in *ghee*.

Nan Griddle bread made with a mixture of wholemeal and self-raising flour.

National income The total money earned within a nation.

Opium A drug derived from a type of poppy.

Papadoms Dry, fried or roasted discs of *urad* or rice flour dough.

Parathas Thick *chapatis*, first baked and then flat-fried in oil.

Parsis Descendants of the Persians who fled to India from Muslim persecution in the seventh and eighth centuries AD.

Pungent Having a very strong smell or taste.

Pullao Spiced rice with vegetables.

Puran-polee A flaky *chapati* stuffed with cooked chickpeas and jaggary.

Purees Circles of wheat flour dough deep fried in oil.

Rasam A hot soup made from soft vegetables and spices.

Retail Shops Shops which sell articles individually, or in small quantities to consumers.

Saffron A yellow substance for flavouring or colouring food.

Sambar A hot soup made from *toor-dal* flour, spices and water.

Samosa A triangular, stuffed savoury pastry, deep-fried in oil.

Sar A thin vegetable soup.

Shira A pudding of semolina, sugar, butter and milk.

Shrikand Thickened yoghurt spread with sugar, saffron and chopped almonds.

Tamarind A sour, bean-like fruit used as a spice when cooking.

Tandoor A clay oven.

Tandoori chicken Chicken pieces spiced and cooked in a tandoor.

Thali A metal serving plate.

Tiffin A light lunch, especially curried dishes and fruit.

Tinders Very small marrows.

Toor-dal Red gram, an important cereal.

Unleavened Bread is unleavened if it is made without yeast, or any other substance to make it rise.

Urad-dal Black gram, an important cereal.

Wholesaler A person or organisation which sells articles in large quantities to retail shops.

Wada A chickpea flour dumpling, stuffed with spiced potatoes and deep fried in oil.

Further reading

For younger readers

Cookery:
Aziz, Khalil, *The Khalil Aziz Book of Simple Indian Cooking* (Evans, 1982)

India:
Barker, Carol, *Arjun and his Village in India* (OUP, 1979)

Jacobsen, P.O., and Kristensen, P.S., *A Family in India* (Wayland, 1984)

Ogle, Carol and John, *Through the Year in India* (Batsford, 1983)

Sandal, Veenu, *We Live in India* (Wayland, 1981)

Zaidee, Lindsay, *India* (A & C Black, 1977)

Commodities:
Blackwood, Alan, *Focus on Grain* (Wayland, 1986)

Blackwood, Alan, *Focus on Tea* (Wayland, 1985)

Religion:
Arora, Ranjit, *Sikhism* (Wayland, 1986)

Al Hoad, Abdul Latif, *Islam* (Wayland, 1986)

Kanitkar, V.P. (Hemant), *Hinduism* (Wayland, 1985)

Mayled, Jon, *Feasting and Fasting* (Wayland, 1986)

For teachers:

Christie, Robert H., *Twenty-two Authentic Banquets from India* (Dover Publications, 1975)

Jaffrey, Madhur, *A Taste of India* (Pavilion Books, 1985)

Kanitkar, V.P. (Hemant), *Hindu Festivals and Sacraments* (The author, 1984). This title is available from Arthur Probsthain, Oriental Booksellers, 41 Great Russell Street, London WC1 B3PH

Koller, J.M., *The Indian Way* (Collier Macmillan, 1982)

Sanderson, F.H., and Roy, S., *Food Trends and Prospects in India* (The Brookings Institution, Washington D.C., 1979)

Shackle, C., *The Sikhs* (Minority Rights Group, 1984)

Shackle, C. (Ed), *South Asian Languages: A Handbook* (School of Oriental and African Studies, London, 1985)

Singh, Balbir, *Indian Cooking* (Mills and Boon, 1984)

Index